Ordinary Impalers

Ordinary Impalers

Poems by

Anton Yakovlev

Kelsay Books

Cover illustration & design by Shay Culligan

ISBN 13- 978-1-945752-31-5

Kelsay Books
Aldrich Press
www.kelsaybooks.com

Acknowledgments

The author is grateful to the editors of the following publications, where these poems first appeared:

Amarillo Bay: "The Submarine"
Blue Monday Review: "The Jogger"
Cardinal Points: "The Immigrant," "Frog Pond," "Many Still
    Speak of Her," "Ordinary Impalers," "The Samurai Season"
Eunoia Review: "I Will Come Back to You as Thunder"
Fulcrum: "Scapegoat Cemetery," "Cliffhanger," "Dance of the
    Sugar Plum Fairy," "The Artist"
The Harvard Advocate: "The Distant Glow of Public Transport"
Long Islander News: "You Could Have Curled Your Brows"
Lunch Ticket: "A Stop Sign Worn as a Helmet"
The Miscreant: "The Music Teacher," "Clearing," "Climate
    Change," "Years Later"
Ohio Edit: "A Celestial Absolute," "The Lingering Portal"
Prelude: "The Visiting Scholar"
Sensitive Skin: "Walking With Difficulty Through the Snow"
The Rutherford Red Wheelbarrow: "Your Last Departing Friend:
    A Self-Portrait," "Sparse Scenery," "The Gallery"

My thanks to Rick Mullin and Donald Zirilli
for their consultation on the manuscript.

Contents

Scapegoat Cemetery

Clutching at gravestones for balance,
he scales the steep hill.

He looks for the grave of the man he can blame
for his inability to talk to you
for the last fourteen years.

He's seen the maps.
He knows where the man is buried.
He's ready to break a goat skull over his headstone.

He cuts across the valley of corporate patsies,
stumbles on the monument to Trotsky.

Sweat soaks his socks.

He wishes he could recall the last time he saw you
and not hear you rage on the phone.

The Submarine

And so you find yourself walking with your father
along the waterfront.
So far you've only exchanged a few syllables.

And you know everything about your father
but imagine he's come back
from a decade in a red light district,
too busy with STDs to pay more attention to you.

There are orphans everywhere,
even those with parents alive,
and there is trash everywhere,
and people pick up the trash
and throw it at each other.

And your father's here,
but still he won't talk,
though the sides of his mouth are moving a little.

You console yourself with the thought that he's just one man
and his name would be Danny Boy in another life
because he's always at war
but still has all those songs going through his head.

Twice a week, the garbage collectors come.
Every year, a useless Christmas is spent
with useless homecomings,
and you act like vampires in withdrawal.

The sides of his mouth say:
Your father is here.
Why can't you talk to him?

And there's a submarine now,
and who knows what it's doing here,
but you both go on and take a tour.
Your father turns out to have a senior pass,
and, besides, it was so boring on land.

Strolling, you almost feel ready to tell him—
not about love, not about your vindictive art—
hell, you never knew what you wanted to tell him about—
and you still don't—
but this evening you almost had it.

Did you want him to show you his footsteps
so you can change their direction?
Did you want him to remember your jokes?
Did you want him to mourn his own father better?

All you'll remember are those wooden plaques
at the spots where the wounded sailors
had fallen during the war,
those painted-over splotches of blood on the walls,
your walls, your father's walls.

You walk with your father through the submarine,
and you know it's the last two hours of alone time
you'll ever get with him—
even if he's alive for many more years—
and somewhere between the deck and the captain's quarters
he opens his mouth and tells you
of some helpful nurse,
some helpful everything,
of pictures of wild horses, of boating,
of chest pains, of chocolate chips.

And you walk alongside him and listen,
and you're the only two people on the submarine,
and nothing in the world will distract you now.

Cliffhanger

By the river, we ask each other,
"When was the last time we had fun?"
and try to build a seesaw with our bodies.

My beard reminds you of a buffalo
sent down by a playful god
and tangled in the cat-infested laundry.

You scratch "REMEMBER INTEGRITY???"
on the side of my Ford Escape.

Our controversial angels take us
into the Hallmark wolf packs,
into the chicken sky.

We leave it to the Vikings to drive
their ATVs across Myles Standish State Forest
and use their blinkers to show us where to turn.

We hold up a bed sheet: a tabula rasa
for the static in the bedroom air.

If someone filmed this, they would cut to
a vulture commercial now.

Dance of the Sugar Plum Fairy

There was always a hint of that classic *Nutcracker* number
in my saunter down Tchaikovsky Street
from my job as a taste-tester at the candy factory Red October
to my second job at the candy factory Bolshevik.
I kept waiting for you to notice that hint.

When you received that genuine Wedgwood bowl
from all those Olympic teams you had led to gold,
did you think of my ballet school diploma,
or my triumphant reports on deluxe dark chocolate bars?

You see, you were never floored by the color
of my hair, you were never floored by the way
I checked my dress in the mirror. You were never floored
by my day-to-day choreography,
by the abandon with which I pounced on the lower octaves
of your candelabraed upright piano.

I knew we would miss our 50-year anniversary.
And I know we won't live to see our 75th.

Still, on that Leningrad white night,
hanging out with your track-and-field team, you tried
to hold on to the chestnut scarf I had dropped,
and though I snatched it from you,
I knew we'd end up together.

Now, after your third stroke,
I could dangle all the scarves I have ever owned
in front of you, and you wouldn't know they were mine.

I could ask you questions to make you figure it out,
make you Sherlock your way to the only reasonable conclusion,
but still it wouldn't click,
just like the description
of a chocolate bar's shape and taste
doesn't make someone blind from birth
understand the color brown.

Sometimes I rush to change your bed sheets,
go down to the laundromat,
come back to hug you,
comb your beard.

Sometimes I go to the store.
You smile: "Don't go!"
I fear those words will be the last I hear,
so I always hurry back home
down Lenin Avenue
with a loaf of bread.

The Immigrant

You bake the pregnant pauses in your small talk,
disarm love in military time,
sprinkle hot sauce in your image
until your solitude becomes a sky.

You threaten the sky with vertigo.

Later, you invite it to dinner.

Oceans huddle in your breast pocket.

—

When you cut film,
your strokes are so severe,
even fresh snow is meat.

Tomorrow you will speak so many languages,
no one will be able to reconstruct
the molecules of your equivocations.

One cannot write enough manuals
to guide anyone through you.

—

Don't talk displacement.
Don't beg for spare infatuation.
Oceans spill out the moment you change your shirt.

Stop fidgeting with your kaleidoscope.
Hold a hand, say hi, have dessert.

Unpack your bags.

It's been twenty years.

Feel the melancholy.

Clearing

Standing in the line-up,
you tilt one side of your mouth
down at the same angle raindrops trace
over Revere Beach
on an especially windy night.

You're one of the foils.
The witness picks out the suspect.
You're dismissed.

A grin lights up your face
like the moon that comes out from behind the clouds
after a storm.

I call you to these line-ups
over and over
just to see that grin.

I can't get it out of you any other way.

Frog Pond

Your parade of suicidal catamarans
cut such an enticing shooting-star
curve in my oubliettes,
I told you I enjoyed spending time with you
in a clearance summer
in a vacuum timetable.

I didn't do a lot of breathing.

But no matter how much you sang,
your teeth were Stonehenge,
or typewriter keys.

My pastor told me your commuter rail
was made of wooden beetles,
so I made myself sleepy.

I was a kettle,
and you an ice cream accident.

Tonight, in a throwback compound,
your flag has shadowed the grass
I'm made of.
You look at me.

Sorry, homey.

Your ghost has solidified.

A Stop Sign Worn as a Helmet

I

He cared for her whimsy
and for the way her shyness played out.

At some gotcha point, in the negative spaces of photos
spotted at some exhibition downtown,
he started to imagine her silhouette,

her T-shirt a burst of yellow
competing with Cape Cod pelicans
and stealthily-erected Jotunheimen high-rises.

She confided in him like a windmill,
invented new flags to lay claim to the territories
they never knew existed.

Everything smelled like good timber,
and the caterpillars grinned friendlier than ever.

He was the road crisscrossing her terraces of abstraction,
the man wrestling with a marlin at the car wash.

She was the mountain centered in his mind
with the slightest suggestion of a dirigible above it.

They hypnotized themselves with each other's choices.

II

Hidden among century-old trees,
surveillance cameras recorded grotesque occurrences,
lined them up in rows,
served them with paprika.

The clouds above the cruise ships
looked like resolute middle fingers
from the shore. It was hard to tell what was going on

with locals hopping from Escher staircase to Escher staircase,
always coming back to the same general tornado.

A half-torn shack blinked satanically with its windows.
Yellow flowers were doors to assorted bad news.
After a while, governments looked like ants.

On the beach, everyone blimped around
with stupid eyes.

He decided he really couldn't be happy
unless a midtown station
demolished in the middle of the last century
rebuilt itself on the double.

A spark in a solar panel started a fire,
but she was too busy long-distance-calling.

The babies who used to hug them wherever they went
looked uncomprehendingly
then fussed.

Sisyphean wrestlers
in a doomed circled wagon,
the two of them finally told their lips
to stop moving.

An unkindness of mockingbirds
marked their generation.

III

Before you meet again,
look for ravens on abandoned rocks
until you realize they are not the point.

The mysteries on which you've given up
are resolved by statues of obscure statesmen
on the Saint Petersburg bridges you've breezed across.

It's almost September,
and the foliage slowly turns into leaf-peeper paradise.
All the church domes are already yellow.

Don't rush back to the garden
where your kiss was stalled
by the sperm-smelling Lower East Side blossoms.

The slouching men you see on the cruise ship decks
are not birds. They won't migrate toward the better,
though they might give you directions yet.

These wires reach beyond the horizon,
where the Sun still makes an appearance,
though a tad morosely.

A rusted ship might float again someday,
if you are nice enough to the bacteria
that captain it from now on.

Climate Change

The sublime, sanctified snow scrubber
from the Stop & Shop where you briefly worked
cleans my car so nicely after the storms.

You work a full-time job developing memes
to combat global warming deniers.

I hear the ocean currents
will shift as the planet warms
and winters will grow only
colder in this part of the country.

Every time I brush the snow off my car,
another plastic thread falls out of the brush.

I gather them the way I used to
gather the loose hairs on the floor
after massaging your head.

Your Last Departing Friend: A Self-Portrait

A midnight run past the school where you used to teach.
Evening kids in a mating dance in tall grass.
Gravestones popping up like dusty old bears.
An undertaker gawks at me as I pass.

At age 18 your brother lifted your skirt, knee-deep in this lake.
You thought nothing of sex: it was a beautiful fall.
Today, in these last days of summer, they call me memory—
chilling near these fences, wearing a hat.

A gargoyle sits on the gates of your concrete town.
The laundromat under your windows is cracking skulls.
Bells ring. Criminals step out into the streets.
Mandibles are knocked out with confident hands.

I am the little man on the upper right of your gates of hell.
A first snow in the plumage of your palms.

The Jogger

Today, when the jogger's days begin
with a tangle of drowsy limbs
and a light dizziness in the shower,
he longs for the days when he was comforted by the whiteness,
running through snow to the bus stop, dollar in hand.
He still travels on the same brown buses each morning
and walks on ice to the train, dodging yellow lights,
but nothing is ahead of him.
Later in the day, his black stapler makes
crocodile noises he never noticed before.

His marriage began as an incensed gallery
of old New England pumpkins, candles in antique stores,
afternoon trips to vegetable farms.
But only autumn could sustain that kind of enchantment.
Quickly he grew to see the void in all other seasons
until autumn, too, turned into an empty wardrobe
where the only spectacle is its fog.

His wife is still perfect to people, but she has skipped
from student to menopause before she turned 30.
She writes online columns eroticizing hotplates,
holds lively conversation about her allergies.
Just like the day they met,
she stares across the river with saintly looks.
Nothing is ahead of them, except death.

And so, today, after postponing it for almost three years,
the jogger travels by train to his old neighborhood
where he first met his wife, running by the river,
and knifes a runner at the exact same location
where he once turned his head and greeted her with

"Excuse me, but I think you're really beautiful
and cannot pass up this chance to run next to you."

Seeing a fountain of near-purple blood
rage through the fence into the river with force,
the jogger becomes confused and runs forward,
just like he should have done many years ago,
without a sound,
when he first noticed his future wife.

He does not stop until it's too dark to run.
On his walk back, there is no body next to the river
and no police cars. Unhindered, he takes the train back.

Returning home, he sees his wife looking out the window,
illuminated by the fireflies outside.
The jogger barely recognizes this person.

He comes upstairs, smiles at her.
She looks at him with taciturn understanding,
shuts the window, and removes his soiled jacket.

Walking with Difficulty through the Snow

I

An old man walked his black dog past a courthouse
on his way toward some memory indicator.
A faint bouquet barely hidden under his coat,
he watched the world with anniversary eyes.

They passed a dry steering wheel next to a wrecked boat.
He penetrated it with his gaze, thinking,
for the two hundredth time today,
that in the end, nothing was cheerful about life.

The courthouse had six windows lit—
a janitor may have been burning death certificates in there,
death certificates from 1942.

The old man reached the graveyard, looked at it in blue:
an angel with his hand under his chin, sadly,
was lost in thinking there, forever lost.

II

With your accountability, you water the trio
of flowers in the mailroom. Sharp blades
of letter openers promise something, never deliver.

For your weaknesses, an earnest raven sends you
free backbones in a twisted ad campaign.

Hard oak doors leave traces on the floor, outlining the semicircles
where people that have fallen took their last breaths.

In 1941, a pallid someone set fire
to this building. He couldn't bear
the sight of people falling.

But the undying human spirit rebuilt it,
then insured itself in church,
on a Sunday, with enduring candlelight.

You know it all but never do anything.
You look under the floor boards and find nothing.

III

And the old man passes by your window, going
home where he leads the life of yesterday's waltz,
bathing his long-dead wife
and putting lipstick on her lips.

Light bulbs on the ceiling shape
the room into familiar parallels.

A candle falls from the desk—and it feels to him
like it's entirely its fault, the blazing burning power,
as if candles *were* time.

The dog no longer smells the wife from his corner.

It is well after dark.

The Music Teacher

Her rigor mortis put everyone on edge.

When Allen and I left her wake,
things came to blows between us
over a song by this star I happened to know,
whose roadie just about beat me up one time
for filming without permission.

Allen just loved that hit single.
Couldn't stand my flippant remarks.

It's been years.

I wonder if he still sits on his porch all day
waving his pretend conductor's baton
at the middle schoolers of Glenwood Landing.

The Visiting Scholar

My head snaps back at the sight
of unafraid geese by the river not getting killed.

You think I'm bored. Actually,
I see amputated limbs in discarded trees.

Sometimes I take out my soccer ball
and meditate on it, reminiscing about the times
I photographed famous players
before they were disappeared.

I imagine my wife's naked body on the park benches.
I might ask you to half-undress
and will be astonished by the thought
that you're unlikely to die in the next two weeks.

I can stare at shadows for hours.
Only black cars fascinate me.

Whenever I see my flag,
I ripple with it.

Many Still Speak of Her

But they all mispronounce her name
to pretend they're speaking of someone else.

Owls turn their heads 180 degrees
to avoid her eyes when she walks by.

She asks for directions, and no one answers.
She just wanders around.

Only a few people have ever touched her,
and those who have scratch at their skin.

It's apple season,
but there are bones in the orchard.

No one remembers her dimples.

The Artist

I

No one approaches her,
so her backpack will stay half-open
until she comes home.

It scratches at her sides
every time she breathes
in the shadow of the statue of Bruckner.

If someone did ask her to dance,
she would pirouette, declawed rose in hand,
spill her soul, then soak it up again.

Some still remember the time
they talked to her on the subway.
Losing her teaches volumes.

She skirts around your oil paintings,
a roaming ghost
once late to the Hades ferry.

A live wire
wrapped in ivy
snakes toward your foot.

A light green parrot,
she flies up to you just before you die
and unplugs the cord.

II

You need to remind yourself that
most backpacks you see on the street
are full of mummified ghosts.

That doctor at the red light
still remembers his father tackling him
to the sounds of Bruckner's Eighth Symphony.

That professor at the wheel
would tell you, if you asked her,
of the day she had to hand in her gun.

Your parents once sat on the subway,
knees almost touching,
planning their sacrifices.

The artist wore green last week
and brushed you with unorthodox silence.
You spent the weekend in Hades.

Meanwhile, a declawed photographer
who would have loved nothing better
than to document your life story

sat at a bar and grill, soaking dollars,
repeating out-of-touch curses
like a pirate whose parrot gave up on him.

III

From the photo, they look at you,
knees almost touching,
subway noise in their eyes.

They've acted in plays together;
now, a toddler blurry from fussing,
you sit in your father's backpack.

Parrots peck at them from the inside.
Cats claw at their lore.
They can barely speak to each other.

She used to look at him
so intensely, he'd look away.
Eventually he learned to meet her gaze.

Now he only sees the photographer.
He can no longer hear Bruckner
in the screeching of subway wheels.

She used to call him Hades.
He used to call her Persephone.
They're afraid they've given up those ghosts.

This photo is thirty years old.
Today, every time he holds out his hand
she clasps it and won't let go.

Years Later

Cameramen rushing in. A summer with its relativistic time.
A standard not followed. A grab bag not full of books.
A velvety melody to calibrate constellations.
The doll with nothing but a record of breasts.

The heavily-taxed forest. A yeti at the screen door.
A young-age fear and the cockroaches used to fight it.
Friendship coexisting, friendship existing,
friendship pretending to spill espresso over its head.

The classic car spitting out humpty dumpties.
The dreamers interrupted by lyme disease.
The exploded fish coming back to explode again.
The unquestionable chasm of a second love.

The no-longer-saintly gambler. The implausible conductor.
The worst chocolate ever filmed. The tree no one mourned.
The rampant adultery of stray dogs.
The exterminator killing with kindness.

The cowboy negotiating pollution. The editor of an elusive lake.
The satellite. The posthumous porch-sitter.
An embalming gone wrong. An excited compass.
The invisible lock in the double door of all ears.

Sparse Scenery

Hard to talk to the embalmed baby
Jesus Christ in his mausoleum.
Winds whirl; all the windows are broken.
Nothing can be heard, except some faraway code.

Quietly, the solemn guardians have left.
Someone will take him away, for sure.
They're already coming, I hear their steps.
His seconds are running out. I ought to rise
to the occasion, I ought to help him.
But blood of faith has handled me pretty roughly,
flows through my veins at many cycles a second,
and I am red. He must take me for a tomato.

The roof is off, and the entire autumn sky
is out here, riding on the baby's back.
The colors are blue and steady. Even so,
they suffer secretly, because they are cold.

Only feelings still remain unfrozen,
and not for long. And I regret already
their disappearance, and I wipe my dry tears.

When I realize the futility of my gesture,
I smile a little. Looking at my hand,
I see brick dust and wonder where it has come from.
But there's really nothing to speak of
all around me, save a bunch of trees
with petty robbers coyly hanging off
the branches, sacks on their heads,
air passing freely in front their noses, but not into them.

They must have been caught before they got a chance
to fulfill their dreams and walk off with Jesus…

But when I look into the mausoleum again,
the baby is gone, and even the sky above him
is nowhere to be found.

                         So I leave my bag
in place of him and walk away, very quiet,
to the rumble of the underground trains.

Ordinary Impalers

You punch a pickpocket to thwart him
then doubt your right to keep your own wallet.

You listen to the sirens on the radio
but get sidetracked by a burp half a block away.

How could you ever hope to glow in the dark?

It's April Fools',
so pretend we can cheer each other,
even if it's Russian Roulette we play.

I'll sip some Poland Spring,
wear my lucky coat,
and walk with you past the cliffs.

Those inclined to solve mysteries
can't help seeing murders around them.
I'll gently wave my hand in front of your face
until you're so dizzy you can't remember *who done it.*

It's not midnight yet. Force your aorta to oxygenate.

Won't you pick up some garbage
from that toppled can
and make origami?

Every time the crosswalk walking man
changes back to a red hand stop,
the festival in your eyes
burns down.

It's Ash Wednesday.

The Distant Glow of Public Transport

Do I fall asleep sniffing in bad figments of doctrine?
People I like flatten themselves
to the waves and patterns that once inspired some
great brain to pummel verbal images on paper.
People I remember drink coffee
with people I don't remember, and I judge
them according to the waves and patterns that once inspired some
great brain to pummel verbal images on paper.

The coffee is sickeningly black, it might as well be
coffee. And he who drinks
it is doing funny little things with his watch.
15 minutes pass, nothing changes. She who drinks too
looks at him, unobtrusively begs him to listen,
and he does, oh yes he does. A man walks out of the bathroom
with toilet paper. The waitress stops him.
She fines him. Later, she will write a poem about him.

You stand by the wall, looking lost and bitter.
At length, this scene is eclipsed by beautiful music
that really gets to the bottom of the afternoon.
You spin an umbrella, and raindrops pour over
windows (in about 6 hours they will be black,
menacing, I will pass by them and turn
away, choosing not to look). Someone else sucks up
his pride and takes your picture despite your dirty look.

He will draw your portrait, beautiful, romantic,
swerving your umbrella in the rain, sad like lilacs.
Then a bus will splash dirt on it, giving you a long
black nose and an extra eye on the forehead.
It's been said love gives people a third eye.

I've got my first and second shut, and see you
in two dimensions, but what a sight you are nevertheless!
(A glutton hurries past. A thin man stumbles.

10 years from now, he will become a senator.)
When I take my next breath, the artist has
already erased your extra eye, and you love me
no more. My own eye weeps, but sticks
around. A web of medieval heraldry resurfaces
on the pages of the great brain. That happened circa 1560.
In 1990, his prophecies were refuted
and he was posthumously sentenced to death.

I remember this and fall asleep with a sense
of great relief. Stray cats are tugging at my coat-tails.
Meanwhile, in another country (impoverished
not too long ago by some wicked bad people) a storm
is gathering and you adjust your collar. You need a friend
to tell you things are fine, but he's been dragged off
to face a firing squad last night. Besides, he wasn't even
your friend. You hum bitterly, and a bus arrives.

The Gallery

I ran into someone who lives in your neighborhood,
and all at once my mind was full of snapshots:
a New Year's in Prospect Park
with fireworks so bright, you wore your sunglasses;
the way you ran from traffic on Flatbush Avenue;
the way you always took the F train by accident;
your flounder shirt that changed color;
the greasy finger that blocked you
in a picture some tourist took;
your almost-mugging and the way you never stopped being scared;
the violin you listened to as intently
as if you wanted to become sound.

We're no longer on speaking terms.
Nothing happened. We've drifted too far apart.
Now it's impossible to be in each other's presence.

But today every piece of art on the wall
reminds me of you
and feels like the first true thing I've noticed in years.

I hear a British folk trio sing about maggots:
a man with no social skills has died,
and no one noticed except the maggots inside him.

I don't care to be social
with anyone but you.

Maybe I'll run into you—
maybe someone will force you at gunpoint
to take part in some poetry reading
where everyone in the audience except me

is an alligator
and you have no choice but to talk to me.

I miss you.

You bust cranberry-filled soap bubbles,
crack the fine points of the Americano,
get in with all the right elephants in the room,
drive your Hyundai Azera,
wake up with a heartache after a heart-to-heart.

Our paths never cross.

A Celestial Absolute

Poem ending with a line by Abbas Kiarostami

Back when you were a cloud, I would raise my eyes,
and right away I kind of knew direction.
When the wind sliced you into two halves,
I knew not where to turn the compass, not what to think,
not how to explain this thing that had come to pass.
I guess you had never been a regular human being,
but I failed to see if this had made you more
or less than. And the mountains told me nothing.

Then a bee flew up to me and stung me.
It was a huge bee: when I tried to hold it,
it fell out of my hands, it was so huge.
Dying in the field, I said: "Holy rusted metal,
will someone play some songs at my funeral?"
They all would, but I kept getting better.
Now I have a shelf-full of sad music
that I still listen to, I really don't know why.

It's playing now. You float across the sky,
one half of you blocking the Southern Cross.
When little bears attacked the weather station
last month, they lost all traces of the other.
For all I know, you may be the cloud outside this window,
or over the graveyard where I go for walks
with my cellphone, because the dead won't hear me.
Once I fell into a grave, and nobody pulled me out.

You used to throw flowers on graves, tenderly recalling
the names of those you knew, buried elsewhere.
You used to milk cows, too, listening to poetry
a stranger told you, but not really listening at all.

You lived in darkness, reaching out for fireflies
as the only means of lighting your way out.
Meanwhile, they had given me stars on a plate,
and my spirit, like a plate, burned out.

Tonight two strangers sleep, separated by a Grand Canyon,
on comfy couches to the sound of apocalyptic static.
Endless poetry runs across the TV screen, and it's all about
bees, bees, bees – plus a sweating scarecrow.
Not an eye moves. And then the blue light cuts in,
the Moon comes out with its wicked axe,
the ballroom floor is enlivened by some death metal…
I thought a lot; and when I left, it had rained.

I Will Come Back to You as Thunder

I will be just out of sight,
just beyond the sun.

But the sun is so twentieth century.

Most of us swim indoors,
or shade our noses.

———

I will be resurrected as a rainbow.

But rainbows' stock has really fallen of late.

Name one person you know
who gives a damn about rainbows.

Well, there *was* that one guy
who had stopped his beater on Highway 287
to take pictures.

———

You will see traces of me in the flight of herons.

Rhodes and Fulbright applicants
do pay attention to herons,
but only while on specially-designed boardwalks.

———

A bald eagle will carry my spirit.

Bald eagles can best be seen
by people who mountain-bike,
but they are generally too busy
ripping their abs.

—

And who the hell cares about thunder?

You can always keep track of the forecast—
that's what your phone is for—
and wait out the rain
at a brewery.

—

Meteors spray the sky
like pieces of silver,
but you are in no mood to even look up.

You walk on,
holding your giant, stone-proof umbrella,
forever faithful to me,
forever alone.

You Could Have Curled Your Brows

I remember the feel of your sideways glance
before you stopped seeing me.
I remember when you didn't cry.

Tonight I will think of your lashes
and their impact on me.
I will nestle behind my couch

eavesdropping on my own vinyl
of the Tchaikovsky birch anthem.
I will imagine your squint.

Hollow theater will avalanche
over my back. Your closed eyes
were always so Sherlock Holmes.

God is a traffic light. You brake
your car. Someone else tunes your radio.
I wish I had opened your door.

The Samurai Season

Move along, nothing more to see here.
The beheadings have all been moved to museums.
We're all here only by the grace of
shutting up—a miniature survival.

Reaching the lookout, you praise the epicurean landscape,
set aside the miserable sticks and stowaways of your child.
You keep readjusting your glow,
you underdog you. In the samurai season, religion
is a kind of ballad, sprinkled with fresh skeletons of birds.

Never mind the pervasive spectacular feathers.
Open your mouth, and the entire forest disappears.

The Lingering Portal

In my dreams, the dogs always devour me
along with whoever got washed up in a trunk
from the sea, who kept me silent company
the morning after the bloody
battle of the captain with the stowaways.
He devours me sideways, while the dogs pull at me
skyward, and in directions I can't name.
They lick their unfeeling lips, they have something on their minds.
They come from far away, carrying long-lost memories,
not thinking as much as feeling, and even that
barely visible behind their black-eyed faces
that smile persistently, disappearing,
melting into the land.

And then I see myself tangled in scarves,
as I walk away somewhere unpleasant
through this tall scenery with bits of dead earth,
serving no purpose other than to walk.
Slowly something rises behind the fog,
and I'm oblivious to its music.
It harmonizes distractedly, shies away
and then envelops me in green.

Further down the path, alleyways watch each other,
tangled in affectionate macabre poses,
shining a cold white light at another lost girl.
She has been staring at these fences so long,
but still they are so difficult to live with.
There is too much emphasis in them,
too much private, unrequited compassion.
Yesterday morning she finally snapped at them,
packed her bags, forgave them and made her plans
for a future that did not include them.

As she makes her way along the shore,
ships pass her by. These ocean liners are left
at the mercy of captains throwing trunks across waves,
each trunk a life, a fullness of cathartic
hopes in their prime. Hungry, they wash ashore,
cuddle with each other, cling to sand,
unable to stand up. And this is where I come in,
walking obliviously in their direction,
penguin-like, and not hearing behind the waves
the barking of those who have been here before me
and look at me. Behind the fences, there is a house;
and behind the blinds of that house, the Sun.
It shines through them, making them feel transparent,
and they show glimpses of the world outside
to the old man who lives in his wheelchair.
He sees the church, he sees the passing clouds
and, thinking of the days past, when somebody's hair
would fly across her face like a spiderweb,
begins to lose his balance and go to sleep.

About the Author

Born in Moscow, Russia, Anton Yakovlev studied filmmaking and poetry at Harvard University. He is the author of poetry chapbooks *The Ghost of Grant Wood* (Finishing Line Press, 2015) and *Neptune Court* (The Operating System, 2015). His poems have appeared in *The New Yorker, The Hopkins Review, Prelude, Measure, The Best of the Raintown Review, The Stockholm Review of Literature,* and elsewhere. His book of translations of poetry by Sergei Esenin is forthcoming from Sensitive Skin Books in 2017. He has also directed several short films.

62271276R00032

Made in the USA
Lexington, KY
02 April 2017